Living
as a
Christian

The Journey Study Series

Searching for Hope

Living as a Christian

Leaving a Legacy

Dealing with Doubt

Confronting the Enemies Within

Embracing the Good News

Building a Christ-Centered Home

Learning to Pray

The Facilitator's Guide

Living as a Christian

A Thomas Nelson Study Series
Based on *The Journey*
by
BILLY GRAHAM

THOMAS NELSON
Since 1798

NASHVILLE   DALLAS   MEXICO CITY   RIO DE JANEIRO   BEIJING

Published in Nashville, Tennessee. Thomas Nelson is a trademark of Thomas Nelson, Inc.

Thomas Nelson, Inc., titles may be purchased in bulk for educational, business, fund-raising, or sales promotional use. For information, please e-mail SpecialMarkets@ThomasNelson.com.

Living as a Christian: A Thomas Nelson Study Series Based on The Journey *by Billy Graham*

ISBN-13: 978-1-4185-1766-3
ISBN-10: 1-4185-1766-6

Printed in the United States of America

07 08 09 10 11 RRD 5 4 3 2 1

Contents

1. Starting Strong / 1
2. Obstacles along the Way / 19
3. It's a Marathon / 39
4. The Call to Discipleship / 59
5. Our Unfailing Guide / 79
6. Traveling Together / 99
Notes / 119

1

Starting
Strong

To get the most from this study guide, read pages 74–77 of *The Journey*.

We weren't meant to be spiritual babies. God's goal for us is spiritual maturity.

BILLY GRAHAM
The Journey

THINK ABOUT IT

I've never been one who thought the good Lord should make life easy; I've just asked Him to make me strong.

—EVA BOWRING[1]

And he died for all, that those who live should no longer live for themselves but for him who died for them and was raised again.

—2 CORINTHIANS 5:15

Babies are interesting. They have little concern for the needs of others, demand their own way, interrupt at will, and are more than happy to let you know when things aren't going their way. We can deal with babies because we realize that their condition is temporary. They grow and mature. Before long, their schedules conform to our schedules. They eat the same food we eat. They can verbalize their concerns rather than simply crying about them.

The same can be said about spiritual babies. Their condition immediately following spiritual rebirth is temporary—we hope! But just like physical maturity, spiritual maturity is a life-long process that involves continual change. The idea is to grow more mature every day. That doesn't happen in the lives of many believers. Why?

REWIND

What keeps you from growing spiritually?

_____ **I'm not interested in growing. I just want to go to heaven when I die.**

_X_ **I'm too distracted by other things.** to listen

_____ **I'm too busy.**

_X_ **Today, I am growing because:**

I am attending church, bible-studies, and studying His word.

What are three things you do to grow spiritually?

Maturity means obedience to ——— God

1. ~~Pra~~ Read Scripture —————

2. Take Online Courses geared toward Christianity

3. Listen to Spiritual people.

We need to grow in many areas of life. If we don't grow in our knowledge of our professions, we suffer the consequences. If we don't grow in our understanding of what it means to be a parent, we suffer the consequences. Likewise, if we don't grow in our spiritual lives, we suffer the consequences.

What are the consequences of spiritual stagnation?

No growth, never realize the potential or experience the plan God has for you. Need to put in the effort to grow.
— feeling disconnected from God.

Like babies, new believers begin their spiritual lives with a dependence on others. They must be taught and trained so that they eventually can stand on their own. The problem is that many believers never move out of the dependence stage. Years after their salvation experiences, they still exhibit characteristics consistent with being spiritual babies.

Read Hebrews 6:1 and 1 Peter 2:2. What is the common message of these two verses?

that we should be striving and
striving for
wanting spiritual growth.

It should be our goal and our

biggest aspiration.

Spiritual maturity is our goal.

If we review the entirety of Scripture, we will find that many of the spiritual struggles faced by God's people were the direct result of spiritual immaturity. The Israelites failed to deepen their relationship with God, so they sinned in spite of God's miraculous work on their behalf. The disciples didn't grow in their understanding of who Jesus was, so they couldn't deal with His death. The list goes on and on until it reaches you and me. Many of our spiritual struggles are directly related to our lack of spiritual maturity. We have remained *carnal,* or "driven by our own desires and lusts."

JOURNEY THROUGH GOD'S WORD

Paul uses the term *carnal* in reference to believers whose earthly desires were greater than their spiritual desires. You might say that people are naturally carnal and subject to the consequences of that life—which is death.

Believers only have two choices about how to live their lives. They will either live carnal lives or spiritual lives. The carnal life is lived contrary to God's laws; the spiritual life is lived in accordance with God's laws. Carnal Christians are often sources of discord within the body of believers. When carnality takes over, the church is in trouble.

The battle between godly desires and fleshly lusts isn't new. Peter encouraged believers to stand strong against their fleshly lusts (1 Peter 2:11) so that they would not misrepresent what it means to be a follower of Christ.

The same battle is being waged today. We see people we know to be Christians doing things that are inconsistent with their faith. Their conversion experience was real; they simply haven't matured beyond the point of allowing their fleshly desires and motives to control their attitudes and actions. The antidote to carnality is spiritual maturity. If believers don't intentionally seek spiritual growth, they will become carnal. There are no other choices.

Remember this world is not our home.

7

RETHINK

On average, how much time do you spend each day in each of the following activities?

Activity	Hours
Sleep	8
Personal care (shower, dressing, etc.)	1
Eating and meal preparation	1.5
Commuting	___
Work	___
Caring for family's needs	___
Hobbies	___
School	2
Computer (other than work and school)	2
Household chores (laundry, yard work)	4
Reading magazines/books	1
Watching television	4.5
Listening to music	___
Other: _____	___
TOTAL	___

What's something you do that isn't on the list?

<u>Hunt, Fish, etc. - Outdoor</u>

<u>Activities</u>

How much time on average do you spend in activities that lead to spiritual growth and maturity? —Not Spending enough time

<u>One Hour</u>

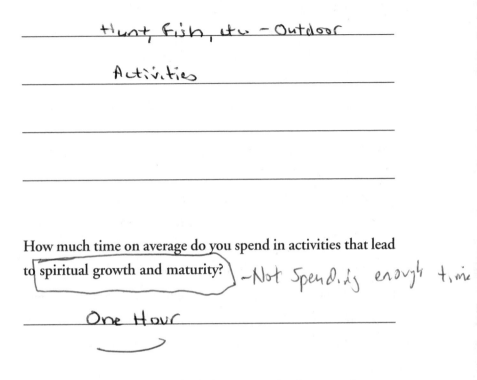

When you analyze your schedule, you might discover that you spend a lot of time in activities that don't produce spiritual growth. If so, you can't expect to grow spiritually. If you are going to grow spiritually, you must be intentional about it; it doesn't just happen because you spend time in church or listen to a sermon during your commute. These are great things to do, but alone they can't enable spiritual growth.

Review the list above and identify some adjustments you can make so that you will have more time available for spiritual

growth. List those adjustments here, and be prepared to review the list regularly.

Spend less time watching television and more time in God's word.

Continue my reading but read more Spiritually centered material.

Is your spiritual life changing from year to year? Think back five years. How has your spiritual life changed since then? Are you still in the same place or have you matured in your relationship with God? Do you have the same spiritual expectations and experiences that you had years ago? Are you going through the motions as if doing so will keep God from zapping you? Many people live this way, and they know what the carnal life is.

You can be sure that Satan delights in an immature Christian. An immature Christian is an ineffective Christian, making little impact for Christ on the lives of others. An immature Christian also is an inconsistent Christ, living for Christ one day and forgetting Him the next. Don't let anything—or anyone—stand in the way of your growth in Christ.
BILLY GRAHAM
The Journey

Rate your life. Where are you and in which direction are you moving? Place an X to represent where you are today, and then draw an arrow representing your direction of movement.

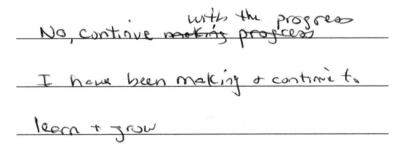

Carnal --------------------- X --------------- Mature

Are you happy with where you are? If not, what is your plan for improving your spiritual life?

No, continue making with the progress

I have been making & continue to

learn + grow

REFLECT

Is there a proven plan for spiritual growth? There are several biblical examples that suggest some things that lead to spiritual growth. One of these examples is found in the believers at Thessalonica. Paul's first experience with these people wasn't so positive. He was forced to flee the town and go to Berea because the Thessalonians fiercely opposed him. Later Paul sent Timothy back to Thessalonica to determine the strength of the church there. Timothy brought back a report that the Thessalonian Christians were surviving in spite of persecution.

The news of the faith of the Thessalonians was spreading throughout the area. There was reason for Paul to send back a letter of encouragement while also responding to some questions the Thessalonians had sent by way of Timothy. Second Thessalonians was written to address concerns about the end times and false teachers.

Within the first chapter of the letter, we see evidence of spiritual growth in the lives of the Thessalonians. As we consider the evidence, we can evaluate our own spiritual growth. Let's look at a few questions to help us evaluate our spiritual maturity.

1. **Is your love for other believers growing?**
   (2 Thessalonians 1:3)
   This was the first evidence Paul mentioned in his letter to the Thessalonians. Christian love isn't self-seeking. So, authentic love results in a desire to make the lives of other people better while pouring out your own life. Is this the way you live? If not, you have some room for spiritual growth.

Are you willing to be inconvenienced so that other people can grow closer to God?

   X Yes   _____ No

Are you looking for ways to make sacrifices so that others might know God better?

__✗__ Yes　　　____ No

2. **Is your faith in God a topic of conversation among other believers?** (2 Thessalonians 1:4–5)
   It's easy to want people to talk about us, but that's not the point here. Paul said that he and his companions talked about the *faith* of the Thessalonians that sustained them through their trials and tribulations.

When life falls apart, what do people see in you?

____ Faith　　　__✗__ Complaints ~~Says Debbie~~ Don't know

When people mention your name, what is their first thought?

__✗__ You　　　____ Your faith

3. **Is God's work your work?** (2 Thessalonians 1:11–12)
   We get this one backwards sometimes. We expect our work to be God's work, but God doesn't conform to our desires. We must take note of what God is doing and then invest ourselves in His work. That is where real fulfillment comes from.

Are you inviting God to get involved in what you've decided to do, or are you looking for ways to get involved in God's work around you?

_____ I'm inviting God to join me.

_X_ I'm joining God in His work.

If you can answer "yes" to the three previous questions about love, faith, and God's work, you are growing spiritually. You can be sure of this because our natural tendencies would force us to answer "no" to these questions. Spiritual growth is the only cause for "yes" answers. But what if you answered "no" to any of the questions? Well, first of all, you should be commended for your honesty. Many people might say "yes" just to feel good about themselves. Acknowledging your spiritual weaknesses is the first step toward spiritual growth. Saying "no" to one question also can help target your solution. You might even have degrees of "yes" and "no" for each question. For instance, you might be close to "yes" in one area and a more certain "no" in another area. So use your responses to help you determine a plan of action.

REACT

In 1 Corinthians 3:1, Paul said, "Brothers, I could not address you as spiritual but as worldly—mere infants in Christ." Take a moment and consider what Paul was saying. Now replace the word *brothers* with your name.

_____Erick_____, I could not address you as spiritual but as worldly—a mere infant in Christ.

Is this statement true about you?

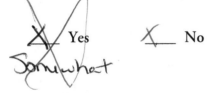

___ Yes   ___ No

Somewhat

This might not be true of you. That's the plan. However, this statement might be truer than you think it is. If so, there is hope. You can start today on the path of spiritual growth by making important the things God says are important and eliminating those things God says are unimportant or distracting. As we will see in the next lesson, the road to spiritual growth is not like an uncrowded interstate highway; there are obstacles to avoid. But for starters, you can do the following.

1. **Commit to spending time with God daily.**
   This isn't just an opportunity to tell Him what He needs to do for you; it is a time to listen to Him by reading His Word and praying.

2. **Focus on allowing God to work through you to meet the needs of someone else.**

   This can be a challenge, but one of the most effective tools for spiritual growth is service.

3. **Spend time reflecting on your day from God's perspective.**

   What were your victories and failures? What can you learn from the day's experiences?

4. **Keep a spiritual journal.**

   This becomes your written testimony. When you have doubts and fears, you will gain strength by remembering what God has done in your life in the past. It also becomes something you can pass on to future generations.

Spiritual growth doesn't happen accidentally; you must be intentional about it. Make today the first day of a new awareness of God's presence in every aspect of your life.

We need all the help we can get to grow and become spiritually mature.

BILLY GRAHAM
The Journey

What are three truths you learned in this study, and how will you apply each truth to your daily life?

1. without continual diligence I could become spiritually stagnant. Make an effort every day to get into God's word.

2. That I need to watch out that I do not become engrossed in my carnal life. — Do not let myself get sucked into following people who are living carnal lives.

3. I cannot attain the spiritual growth I am looking for without adjusting my schedule by — using my time more wisely and in God's word.

In the Program:
→ Remove the Barriers

2

Obstacles
along
the Way

T O GET THE MOST FROM THIS STUDY GUIDE, READ
pages 77–82 of *The Journey.*

> *Don't let anything—or anyone—stand in the way of*
> *your growth in Christ.*
>
> BILLY GRAHAM
> *The Journey*

THINK ABOUT IT

If you find a path with no obstacles, it probably doesn't lead
anywhere.

—FRANK A. CLARK[1]

My prayer is not that you take them out of the world but
that you protect them from the evil one.

—JOHN 17:15

Do you ever wish that God would just remove you from the trap-
pings of the world so that you could focus your full attention on

Him? Even though we can't do that now, there is a day coming when we will do nothing but focus on God. At least those who know Jesus Christ as personal Lord and Savior will have that privilege. Until then, we must pursue spiritual growth while living in this world. No matter how strong your faith, that isn't an easy task!

Why don't we grow in our faith? There are plenty of reasons. The main reasons, however, are that most Christians don't realize that they need to grow or they don't know how to grow. Some people only see the eternal effect of salvation—admission to heaven—while overlooking what salvation means while they are here on earth.

REWIND

When you consider salvation, which aspect is your primary focus?

_____ **Where I'm going when I die**

_*x*_ **What it means while I'm alive**

What are three things that have interfered with your ability or desire to grow spiritually? *Being a follower*

1. _People - falling in with non-spiritual people._

2. _Places - going to places a spirited person doesn't belong_

3. _Things - alcohol, elicit material_

Obstacles are a part of life. We encounter them while shopping, driving, working, and worshiping. Sometimes it's easy to overcome the obstacles, but at other times, they seem to overwhelm us. Have you ever been stuck in a traffic jam and turned back rather than continue with your trip? Have you ever had to change the plans for a project because there were too many objections to the original plans? These are examples of obstacles and how you might have reacted to them.

But what about spiritual obstacles? You can be certain that many of the spiritual obstacles you face are the work of Satan. If your obstacles make you turn back, then you are virtually ineffective for God. That's exactly what Satan wants to do to you.

Read John 10:10. What are the two conditions presented by Jesus in this verse? _–Just a guess_

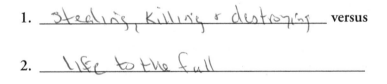

1. _Stealing, killing & destroying_ **versus**

2. _Life to the full_

Immature Christians often are the reasons some unbelievers choose to remain that way. We don't have to look very far to see someone claiming to be a Christian living contrary to the principles of their faith. The problem of spiritual lethargy isn't limited to new believers. Matter of fact, some might argue that new believers are far more committed to spiritual growth than are veteran believers.

Compare your present commitment to spiritual growth with your commitment when you were a new believer. Are you more or less committed to growth? Explain the change.

More, because now I have a better grasp on the things that make a good christian and know that my relationship with Jesus is first and foremost.

JOURNEY THROUGH GOD'S WORD

What is a disciple? In the New Testament, the term generally is used to refer to followers of Jesus Christ (although sometimes it was used specifically in reference to the twelve men who accompanied Jesus during His three-year ministry). The term can be translated as "pupil" or "learner."

In the first century, most teachers and philosophers had disciples under their leadership. This was one of the primary ways that ideas were distributed. There were no media outlets to assist with spreading new ideas. The processes used by those teachers still are part of our educational philosophies today—question and answer, repetition, and memori-

---

zation. Eventually, the student would become a teacher leading a new generation of students.

This model of discipleship has been handed down from generation to generation and is still an effective way for people to grow spiritually. However, the problem today is that people won't commit the time necessary for this type of growth. We want learning to be fast and neat, yet discipleship is slow and sometimes messy.

In the New Testament, the term *disciple* appears 261 times and is confined to the four gospels and the book of Acts. In true Jewish form, Jesus often was referred to as "Rabbi" or teacher. Disciples had the option of choosing their teachers. Therefore, many followed Jesus but never became His students. The same is true today. Following Jesus means living by His standard—a standard that He exhibited in His daily life. Jesus' disciples included a large gathering of people of all types. It was from the larger body of followers that He selected the twelve who were closest to Him. The term *apostle* generally refers to those who were eyewitnesses of Jesus after the Resurrection. Therefore, Paul was qualified to be called an apostle. *Disciple* became a term that generally applied to all believers. It is synonymous today with the term *Christian.*[2]

RETHINK

Rate the following obstacles based on the degree of trouble you have with each one, with 1 being no problem and 5 being a major obstacle.

Activity	Rating
Household chores	1
Work	5
Friends and family	$2
Recreation	1
Sporting events	1
Hobbies	1
Other: _____	_____

Based on your responses, what do you think are the two biggest obstacles to your spiritual growth?

Work, Friends + Family

We need to remind ourselves that God didn't leave us here for our purposes; He left us here for His purposes. And one of His purposes is that we grow more and more like Christ.

> *What is spiritual maturity? To put it another way, what exactly does God want to do in our lives as we journey along His path? The Bible gives us the answer: God's will is for us to become more and more like Christ. It is that simple—and also that complex. This is spiritual maturity, and if you make this your goal, it will change your life.*
>
> BILLY GRAHAM
> *The Journey*

Read 2 Peter 3:18. How would you characterize Peter's words?

_____ They are a good idea.

_____ They are a suggestion for people who have the time.

__X__ They are instructions for everyone.

Read Romans 8:29. According to this verse, to whose image are we to be conformed?

_____ Jesus likeness _____

We don't have to wonder about God's will for our lives; He has already told us that His will is that we become more and more like His Son. In becoming like Jesus Christ, we will discover the activities in which God wants us to invest ourselves. God's will for you is not summed up in a vocation; your vocation is the way God provides for you to carry out His will.

REFLECT

What is the key to spiritual maturity? First, you have to begin by understanding that spiritual growth isn't just for a few spiritual giants who have huge Bibles and nothing else to do but sit around reading them. That's not the way it is. God wants you to become more like Christ right where you are. Jesus didn't isolate Himself from everyday life; He lived in the midst of the same culture in which His followers lived. He knew the struggles they faced. He knew what it was like to have everything and everyone pulling against God's leadership in His life. Maybe you can relate.

What are the daily pressures you face?

Financial, trying to rid myself of the

thoughts that are displeasing to God,

job search related

How do these pressures affect your desire to grow spiritually?

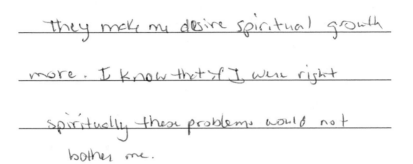

_they make my desire spiritual growth
more. I know that if I were right
spiritually these problems would not
bother me._

Jesus withdrew from public life in order to be spiritually renewed. He spent time in prayer and fasting, but He didn't allow His renewal to disconnect Him from the public. That is the danger we must avoid. We can spend so much time in our "holy huddles" that we have no relevance in the world. That is why Jesus said, "My prayer is not that you take them out of the world" (John 17:15).

Which statement best characterizes your spiritual relationship with the world?

_____ I am a positive spiritual influence on the world.

__X__ I am letting the world influence my spiritual life.

_____ I am not sure.

One of the statements above is true about each of us. We are either being spiritual influences on the world or we are being

29

influenced spiritually by the world. It is clear as to the desired response—being a positive spiritual influence on the world. But how do we make that a reality in our lives?

> *Don't take lightly what it means to submit every area of your life to Christ's authority. Take your body, for example. God gave it to you—but do you allow its desires to control you? Or what about your mind? Or think about your motives. What about your tongue? The list could go on and on: our relationships, our finances, our attitude toward those of another race, our concern for those in need, our emotions—everything. Never forget: God's will is for us to become more like Christ—and this only happens as we submit every area of our lives to His authority.*
>
> BILLY GRAHAM
> *The Journey*

1. **Daily submit every area of life to His authority** (Luke 9:23).

   God doesn't invade our space and take over our lives; we must submit to Him. But submitting isn't a selective process. We must give every area of our lives to God without holding back.

What areas of life are the most difficult for you to turn over to God? Why?

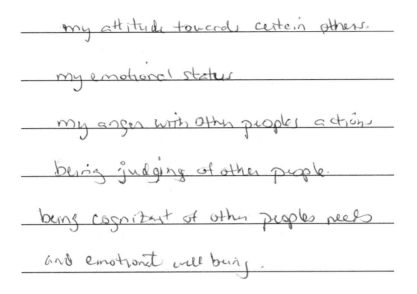

my attitude towards certain others.

my emotional status

my anger with other peoples actions

being judging of other people.

being cognizant of other peoples needs

and emotional well being.

It is easy to rejoice in what we get when we are saved, but how easy is it to rejoice in what we get to give? When you gave Christ your life, did you specify certain aspects of life? Were your terms of salvation conditional? Certainly not! If you didn't offer Christ all of your life, you didn't offer any of your life to Him.

But old habits are hard to break. So as we move through life, our salvation experience is in the distant past. Those old habits return and we are left wondering just what happened to our spiritual lives. The solution is found in daily submitting our lives to Christ.

Read Luke 9:23. What are the three actions that are required of believers?

1. <u>deny yourselves</u>

2. <u>take up the cross daily</u>

3. <u>follow Jesus</u>

Spiritual lethargy is the end result of not daily submitting every area of life to God. When we hold back, we prevent the Holy Spirit's efforts to change our lives from the inside out.

Consider the following areas of your life. To what degree does God daily control each area? (1=not at all, 5=completely)

Your body and its desires	1	2	3	(4)	5
Your attitude toward others	1	2	(3)	4	5
Your thoughts	1	2	(3)	4	5
Your behavior with others	1	2	3	(4)	5
The words you speak	1	2	(3)	4	5
The things you read and watch	1	2	(3)	4	5
The music you listen to	1	2	3	(4)	5
The way you handle money	1	2	(3)	4	5
Your attitude toward possessions	1	2	(3)	4	5

2. **Involve God in the battle for your will** (John 3:30).
   Your will can be described with the determination
   with which you live each moment. At any point in
   your day, you can choose to obey or disobey God.
   Satan prefers disobedience; God prefers obedience.
   When John the Baptist spoke the words in John 3:30,
   he was insisting that he had to decrease in popularity
   and Jesus' popularity must increase. In the passage,
   John went on to say that Jesus should be exalted
   because of His divine origin and divine teaching.
   John understood that his role was to point people to
   Jesus Christ.

What is your main focus in life?

____ Point people to Jesus Christ.

____ Attract attention and popularity for yourself.

_X_ Probably a bit of both.

Think about the way you live each day. Are your actions consistent with John's words? Why or why not?

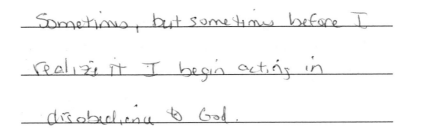

Sometimes, but sometimes before I realize it I begin acting in disobedience to God.

Spiritual growth must be intentional. If you don't choose to grow, you have made a choice not to grow. But choosing to grow is only part of the decision; you also must choose to obey. This is where the battle of the will intensifies. Satan isn't too concerned about your decisions; he is more concerned about your commitments. How determined are you to live each moment for Christ? Unless you turn to Him for strength, your efforts will be in vain.

3. **Embrace the new life** (John 15:11).

   The life of faith is more than a list of things you can't do; there is incredible freedom associated with living for God. The people who followed Jesus noticed what He did, not what He didn't do. They saw in Him a way of life that they wanted. They saw real peace and joy. They saw victory over temptation. They saw life lived for more than earthly rewards.

So many of the things we strive for were not a part of Jesus' life. Use the list below to identify the differences between the focus of your life and the life of Jesus. For each item on the list, place a check in the columns of the individuals who have made it a top priority.

	Jesus	Me
Finances	____	✓
Peace	✓	____
Possessions	____	✓
Popularity	____	✓
Career	____	✓
Leading others to God	✓	____
Pleasing God	✓	✓
Obedience to God	✓	ð·✓
Appearance	____	✓
Retirement	____	✓
Prayer	✓	✓

If you have been on your faith journey for a while, you probably can look back to the changes that can be directly attributed to God's work in your life. Take a few moments to reflect and thank God for what He has done. Ask Him to continue to work to change you in other areas of your life.

Pause for Quiet Prayer Time.

REACT

Many people seek spiritual change from the outside in. That is, they try to act or look spiritual hoping that someday the inner change will come. But that's not the way it happens. Spiritual change begins on the inside.

Read Romans 12:2. What is it that God wants to renew in you?

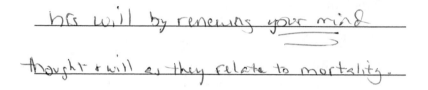

his will by renewing your mind

thought + will as they relate to mortality.

What is the end result of this renewal?

____ Prosperity

____ A job promotion

_X_ An awareness of God's will

____ Popularity

The answer is obvious; you will gain an awareness of God's "good, pleasing and perfect" will. It is good because it is of God. It is pleasing because it is the thing for which you were designed. It is perfect because you need nothing more. Is this your desire?

Rewrite Romans 12:2 as a prayer for your life. Make this prayer a part of your everyday experience.

Heavenly father, give me the strength to no longer be swayed by the evil and corruption in this world and to grow spiritually and morally into the person who ~~conforms~~ is pleasing to God, Amen

> *Don't let another day go by without committing yourself*
> *to God's great plan for you: to be more and more like Jesus.*
> BILLY GRAHAM
> *The Journey*

What are three truths you learned in this study, and how will you apply each truth to your daily life?

1. _As long as I allow obstacles to get in the way, my spiritual growth will be hindered - make finding time for spiritual fulfillment a top priority_

2. God didn't leave us here for our purposes but to grow more like Christ. Try to remember that without Jesus our lives have no meaning.

3. Without submitting all aspects of my life to God I will become spiritually lethargic. Do not apply spiritual principles to only half my life, or pick + choose which areas to turn over to God.

3

It's a Marathon

T O GET THE MOST FROM THIS STUDY GUIDE, READ
pages 85–89 of *The Journey*.

> *The journey that God has given us isn't a sprint but*
> *a marathon.*
>
> BILLY GRAHAM
> *The Journey*

THINK ABOUT IT

Mere change is not growth. Growth is the synthesis of change
and continuity, and where there is no continuity there is no
growth.

—C. S. LEWIS[1]

Therefore, since we are surrounded by such a great cloud
of witnesses, let us throw off everything that hinders and the
sin that so easily entangles, and let us run with perseverance
the race marked out for us.

—HEBREWS 12:1

We live in a time of instant everything. Matter of fact, it seems as if we get more and more annoyed if we have to wait. Do you remember a time when the news came on once a day and lasted only thirty minutes? Back then, a car loan took days to process; a mortgage took weeks. We didn't have microwaves, video recorders, or computers. Communicating meant writing and mailing a letter or picking up the phone to make a call.

Believe me, I'm delighted with our modern advances. Many of the day's processes have been streamlined so that we are more efficient than we used to be. But there is one thing that can't be streamlined—spiritual growth. People have tried to shorten the time it takes to mature spiritually, but it hasn't worked. The truth is, it will never work!

REWIND

Consider your spiritual training to date. Based on your commitment to training, for what are you prepared?

_____ A spiritual marathon

_____ A spiritual sprint

_____ A spiritual jog

__X__ A slow spiritual walk

_____ A seat in the stands as a spiritual spectator

It might not be true of you, but the faith community has its share of spiritual spectators, walkers, and joggers. Occasionally, a spiritual star will sprint through our midst. Yet the real spiritual giants often are unnoticed. They are the spiritual marathon runners. They understand that this journey toward spiritual maturity requires a consistent commitment to life-changing training. Our spiritual lives can't be popped into the microwave or fast-tracked. The spiritual life is one of endurance.

Read Hebrews 12:1–2. When you read the word *endurance*, what images come to mind?

Jesus on the cross

In your spiritual life, what have been some of the things you have endured?

alcoholism, the influences of non-spiritual people, a family who is very far from spiritual.

Like the marathon runner, we are in it for the long haul. Our journey—our race—lasts as long as God gives us life, and we aren't meant to wander off the track, or quit and join the spectators, or decide we'll just slow down and take it easy while others pass us by. Nor are we meant to collapse from exhaustion in the middle of the race, our strength gone and our reserves drained. God didn't intend for us to travel our journey in our own strength anyway, but only with the strength He supplies.

BILLY GRAHAM
The Journey

When we think back to a time when our faith was new, we probably realize we ran the spiritual course much faster. Maybe it was spiritual adrenaline or pure excitement that caused us to be more aggressive about spiritual growth. But, as life began to happen, the spiritual energy began to wane. What once had been a sprint slowed to a crawl; some people even stopped altogether.

What are some things you do to build your spiritual strength?

Daily prayer
read the bible, go to church, attend th BBSG
bible study, hang around christians
whenever possible, listen to Christian music

JOURNEY THROUGH GOD'S WORD

In the Christian world, we use a lot of words that we don't fully understand. *Witness* is one of those words. We generally use *witness* to describe someone who has experienced something. The degree of involvement of the witness in the experience can vary.

In the faith community, a witness is one who is convinced of and willing to stake his or her life on the truthfulness of events and/or tenets that cannot be proven. There have been situations in which a person died for such beliefs. These people usually are referred to as martyrs. The only difference between a witness and a martyr is the outcome of the testimony.

Throughout Scripture, *witness* has a number of uses that include legal, personal, and evangelistic. In the legal sense, witnesses give testimony as to the validity of factual information. For instance, Numbers 5:11–15 details the legal situation related to an unfaithful wife. In John 20:30–31, Jesus is identified as the personal witness of God's love. In this situation, being a witness is best understood as one's reputation. Therefore, Jesus personified God's love and, through His life, was a witness. The evangelistic use of witness can be found in numerous places in the New Testament including Acts 2:14–47. In this passage, Peter encourages his audience to accept God's offer of salvation.

Being a witness is more than simply speaking words; it is living out your faith and letting your life be a reflection of God's love. Only then are we truly living as witnesses.[2]

RETHINK

What are some of the things you do in a hurry?

drive

How is your attention to detail affected by hurrying?

_____ I can be just as detailed as if I'm not hurrying.

_____ I miss a few details when I'm in a hurry.

__X__ I don't pay much attention to detail when I'm in a hurry.

You might be able to hurry to get the grass cut or prepare a meal. You might even be able to hurry through some assignments at school or work. Hurrying through spiritual growth, however, isn't something you can do without suffering the consequences.

Read Hebrews 5:12–14. What is the primary problem being addressed by the author of Hebrews?

_____ The readers weren't going to church enough.

_____ The readers weren't acting spiritual.

__X__ The readers weren't growing spiritually.

Sometimes we get the order of these options all mixed up. We believe that going to church will make us grow spiritually. Yet, in reality, growing spiritually is a function of your relationship with God. The church can support you in your relationship with Him, but the church isn't a substitute for that relationship.

REFLECT

Any significant accomplishment is a product of a variety of situations and people who have contributed to our lives. The same is true about spiritual growth. You grow in response to the situations you face and the people you encounter. Not every situation that leads to spiritual growth is a positive situation.

Describe a struggle that has produced spiritual growth in your life.

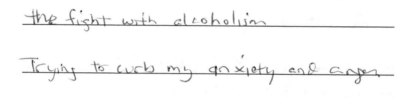

the fight with alcoholism

Trying to curb my anxiety and anger

Maybe you would never willingly choose to go through that situation again, but you can't deny the spiritual growth it produced. Maybe a sudden job loss led you to a new job that enables you to invest your skills in something that makes an eternal difference in the lives of your clients or customers. The job loss was tough, but you can see the personal spiritual growth you experienced along the way. The same might be said about a relationship, a family situation, or a financial struggle.

Why don't we grow through our difficulties? Too many times we seek instant escape from unpleasant situations. If we have a financial problem, we borrow the solution before we learn the lesson. We dissolve relationships before we take time to seek reconciliation. We change jobs before we let God work through the jobs we have. The list of instant solutions goes on and on.

We also don't grow through our problems because we focus on ourselves rather than others. The "woe is me" attitude is easy to develop when we face problems. Yet many times, along with the problem, God provides someone to whom He wants us to minister. But we miss the opportunity because we are too focused on ourselves.

We also don't grow through our problems because we make the mistake of always interpreting our problems as a sign of spiritual failure. Thinking this way is a function of bad theology. The Bible is full of examples of righteous people who suffered. In their suffering, their faith remained strong and their testimony detailed God's faithfulness. How can you respond to difficulty this way? Let's take a look at Philippians 1:27–30 to discover a pattern we can follow.

1. **Let your commitment to Christ guide your conduct** (Philippians 1:27a).
   For Paul, conduct was a responsibility of citizenship. But Paul always emphasized the responsibilities of heavenly citizenship above those of earthly citizenship.

What are your responsibilities as a Christian?

To follow Jesus Christ and live
life using His principles and following His
example.

What are your earthly citizenship responsibilities?

To love thy neighbor and fellow men
To spread the word of God by giving
our testimony
To vote, pay taxes, work

Is it ever difficult to negotiate the tension between these two types of responsibilities? If so, why? If not, how do you negotiate the tension?

Yes, because of men's sin nature
we are constantly being tested.

2. **Seek the support of other believers** (Philippians 1:27b).

   Paul told the Philippian Christians to be one in spirit and in mind as they worked together for their faith. As believers, we need each other. When we encounter problems, we can grow through them by seeking counsel from others who have experienced similar problems. This means we must get to know other believers.

In your spiritual life, how do you get to know other believers?

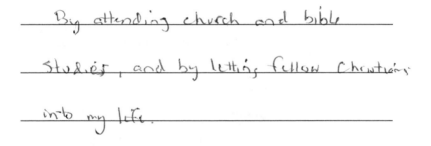

By attending church and bible
Studies, and by letting fellow Christians
into my life.

Name three Christian friends you could turn to if you had a problem.

Debbie, Dennis, + Ginger

What prevents Christians from establishing and maintaining friendships with other believers?

X___ Lack of trust

X___ Unwillingness to be transparent with others

X___ Fear that they won't understand

___ Other: _un willing to reach out_
& express myself (feelings) Strangers

3. **Focus on God, not on your problems** (Philippians 1:28–30).

   Satan would love nothing more than for you to be so concerned about your problems that you stop paying attention to God's work in your life. Paul instructed the Philippians to not be afraid of their adversaries, but to remember God's grace, love, and mercy. The word *terrified* is a strong term used to describe someone being overwhelmed with terror at the sight of his or her enemies. In their efforts to support one another, the Philippians would become legal proof of God's power. This legal proof is the same as "witnesses" described earlier in this lesson.

By watching you deal with your problems, others develop their concepts of God. Maybe you've seen someone suffer a terrible loss and stand strong in their faith. You also might have seen a fellow Christian completely lose control while dealing with a problem. That response paints a picture of God that is inconsistent with the first picture.

Maybe now you see how important it is for God's people to see Him rather than their adversaries.

What "adversaries" regularly attack you?

Financial problems, non-spiritual people and thinking, other drivers on the road

myself — angry, selfishness

What is something you can do to remind yourself of God's ability to help you grow through your problems?

Keep myself surrounded with spiritual People & the Bible, and remind myself that the only reason were in this world is to glorify God.

53

Life's problems will never go away, and you probably will never grow to the point that you look forward to them. However, you can grow to the point that you see God's hand even through the problems. That's what Paul wanted for the Philippians and what God wants for you.

REACT

Spiritual growth isn't an end in itself; it is a process. Though it has a beginning (salvation), it doesn't have an end. There is no point in life when a believer can honestly say, "I have succeeded in maturing in my faith, and I no longer need to learn anything or improve in any area."

Spiritual growth is a marathon that requires strength and determination. Read the following Scripture passages and write down what God is saying to you through each one.

Philippians 4:13

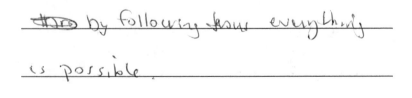

by following Jesus everything
is possible.

2 Chronicles 15:7

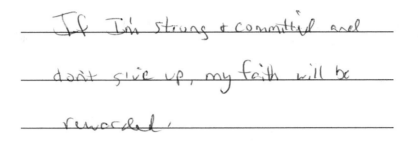

If I'm strong & committed and don't give up, my faith will be rewarded.

Isaiah 35:4

Do not fear for god is coming

1 Corinthians 16:13

Stand firm in your faith

Ephesians 6:10–13

Stand firm against satan.

As you can see, the Bible offers a lot of encouragement to people who are facing trouble. God knew in advance that we would need these words and this degree of encouragement. As you read the Scripture, make note of passages or verses that are of significance to you. Commit these Scriptures to memory so that you can recall them in the midst of your trials.

God's desire is that we be in such a close relationship with Him that we automatically draw on His strength to overcome our struggles. In doing so, He will be honored and glorified and those who doubt Him will see evidence of His presence in the lives of those who call Him Lord.

> _God didn't intend for us to travel our journey in our own strength . . . but only with the strength He supplies._
> BILLY GRAHAM
> _The Journey_

What are three truths you learned in this study, and how will you apply each truth to your daily life?

1. _____

_____

_____

_____

2. _____

_____

_____

_____

3. _____

_____

_____

_____

4

The Call
to
Discipleship

To get the most from this study guide, read pages 89–93 of *The Journey*.

It is no accident that the words discipline and disciple resemble each other in the English language, for they come from the same Latin root. The most common word in the Gospels for a follower of Christ is "disciple," and discipleship cannot be separated from both commitment and discipline. To be a disciple is to be committed—committed to Jesus Christ as our Savior and Lord and committed to following Him every day. To be a disciple is also to be disciplined—disciplined in our bodies, disciplined in our minds, disciplined in our souls.

BILLY GRAHAM
The Journey

THINK ABOUT IT

The Savior is not looking for men and women who will give their spare evenings to Him or their weekends or their years of retirement. Rather He seeks those who will give Him first place in their lives.

—WILLIAM MACDONALD[1]

To the Jews who had believed him, Jesus said, "If you hold to my teaching, you are really my disciples. Then you will know the truth, and the truth will set you free."

—JOHN 8:31–32

The call to salvation and the call to discipleship are intertwined. To experience salvation without discipleship would be the same as experiencing physical birth but never growing up. Being born physically initiates unstoppable growth process. Being born spiritually also initiates a maturing process. So, why are there so many immature believers?

There are many statements in the Bible that begin with *if.* This little word indicates that there is a choice to be made. "Jesus said, 'If you hold to my teaching, you are really my disciples'" (John 8:31). The choice here has to do with making a commitment to the teachings of Jesus. Jesus stated it in the positive, but take a moment to look at it from the other side. The implication is that not committing to Jesus' teachings is making the choice not to be His disciple. Disciple isn't a title; it's a way of life.

REWIND

Think back over the last twelve months. Plot your spiritual growth on the chart that follows.

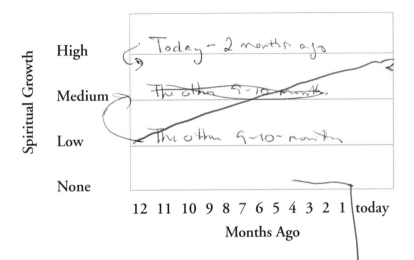

Spiritual Growth

High

Medium

Low

None

12 11 10 9 8 7 6 5 4 3 2 1 today

Months Ago

Handwritten on graph: Today - 2 months ago

Handwritten: The other 9-10 months.

Handwritten: The other 9-10 months

What were the significant events that produced the highest rate of spiritual growth?

returning to church → getting involved and bible study.

What was happening during the times that you experienced the lowest rate of spiritual growth?

No work being done other than my school work,

The discipleship idea has been around for a long time. Early philosophers taught small groups of students the basic tenets of their philosophies. Simply put, a disciple is the same as a learner. Jesus had disciples, as did John the Baptist, the Pharisees, and other teachers of the day. Believe it or not, you have disciples.

List the names of the people who learn from you.

Dylan + Debbie.

_____

_____

In addition to having disciples, you also are a disciple.

List the names of the people from whom you learn.

Dennis, Debbie, Vince, Dylan, Debbie,

+ Charlie.   Jesus

_____

You might not be a student in the classical sense, but you are influenced by a number of people from many walks of life. Fashion designers influence what you wear. Athletes influence your shoe decisions. Celebrities, musical artists, business leaders, politicians, and more all exercise some degree of influence on our culture. But what about Jesus? Does He really have any influence on your daily life? Your honest answer to that question is our main concern today.

JOURNEY THROUGH GOD'S WORD

Throughout history, education has been a part of almost every culture. Most of the teaching that took place in biblical times was informal; that is, it was not held in an established school. The primary topics of discussion were religion and morality. Many of the early biblical instructions were part of this training. Formal education was a privilege afforded the upper class of society.

With the spread of the written Word of God came the need for more formalized training for the general population. The synagogues were often the site for such training for portions of society. The home, on the other hand, always has been the primary venue for religious education.

The Bible identifies three major types of education—informal, semiformal, and formal. Informal education was a function of the home and was the primary way in which parents would train their children in matters of faith and morality. Semiformal education was primarily literacy training carried out by the scribes. Formal training was reserved for society's elite and was managed by hired teachers or slaves. This model of centralized learning was the foundation for the expansion of the Greek philosophical movement.

Paul and Luke almost certainly had some degree of formal training. Paul was a student under the great Jewish teacher Gamaliel in Jerusalem. Luke was a physician, so he likely had some formal training also.

The bottom line is that the basic setting for educating children in matters of faith and morality was and remains the home. The church provides support for the education of children and adults. However, it is not the sole responsibility of the church to train children in matters of faith and morality. Proverbs 22:6 reminds parents to "train a child in the way he should go, and when he is old he will not turn from it."

RETHINK

What have been your most significant spiritual learning experiences? Who have been some of your spiritual teachers?

Through AA and conversations with
Dennis and Debbie. - Dennis, Debbie, Vinie,
Dave, Keith, Gerz.

How would you rate yourself in the area of discipleship?

_____ A: I've got perfect scores in spiritual growth.

X B: I'm above average.

Between

X C: I'm average.

_____ D: I'm hanging on.

_____ F: I'm not growing spiritually.

The same word translated as "if" also can be translated as "since." When we make this shift, Jesus' words in John 8:31–32 take on a more intense meaning:

> _To the Jews who had believed him, Jesus said, "Since you hold to my teaching, you are really my disciples. Then you will know the truth, and the truth will set you free."_
>
> —JOHN 8:31–32

What does it mean to abide in God's Word? To abide is to stay in place. Therefore, abiding in God's Word can be stated as staying put in God's Word. So, Jesus' words in the verse above indicate that staying put in God's Word is foundational to discipleship. Too many times we mistake studying a book about the Bible for studying the Bible. Certainly there are many resources that can be used to enhance our Bible-study experience, but books can't replace The Book!

How much time each day do you spend studying God's Word?

_____ None

_✗_ 1–10 minutes

_____ 11–30 minutes

_____ 31–60 minutes

_____ More than an hour per day

If you spent the same amount of time focusing on your job or your home, how successful would you be?

_____ Not very. _____

_____

_____

Why is it so hard to commit daily time to studying God's Word?

_____ Because life gets in the way, _____

Earthly Responsibilities + Laziness _____

_____

REFLECT

Being a first-century disciple was nothing unusual. That's the primary way that religion and philosophy were promulgated. Some people were uncommitted followers; some were committed disciples. There is a difference!

Describe the difference between a follower and a disciple.

A disciple purpose is to not only follow Jesus but to learn from Him. Discipleship involves a personal relationship

> *The twelve whom Jesus called to be His closest companions were with Him day and night. They had a personal relationship with Him—walking with Him, eating with Him, sharing in His conversation, observing the way He lived, listening to Him preach to the crowds. But they weren't following Jesus just to enjoy His presence. They had a purpose: to learn from Him—absorbing His teaching, learning from His example, even profiting from His rebukes. To be a disciple is to be a learner.*
>
> BILLY GRAHAM
> *The Journey*

First, a disciple is a learner or a student. For those men who were closest to Jesus, learning from Him was a way of life, not a selected activity for a short period of time. The disciples had a personal relationship with Him.

What are the key ingredients in a close personal relationship?

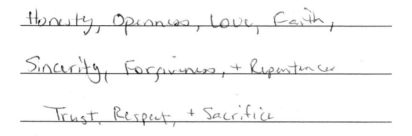

Honesty, Openness, Love, Faith, Sincerity, Forgiveness, + Repentance Trust, Respect, + Sacrifice

In regard to your relationship with Jesus, rate yourself in terms of how close that relationship is (1=poor, 5=excellent). Explain your answer.

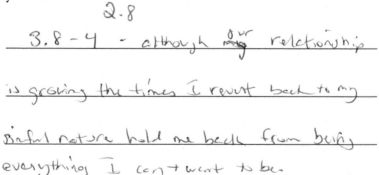

2.8

3.8 - 4 - although my relationship is growing the times I revert back to my sinful nature hold me back from being everything I can't want to be.

Adults choose to learn those things that make a difference in their lives. So, why wouldn't someone choose to learn Scripture? Maybe they don't perceive it to be something that might make a difference. They might view Scripture as a list of rules meant to rob them of all of the things they enjoy. Nothing could be more untrue. There is incredible freedom within the boundaries of our faith.

Read the following Scripture passages looking for the common theme.

> Psalm 119:45
>
> Isaiah 61:1 ~ 𝓺𝓹
>
> Romans 8:20–21
>
> 2 Corinthians 3:17
>
> James 1:25

Depending on the translation you used, you discovered that liberty or freedom is a common theme that runs throughout Scripture. This is one of the basic facts of our faith. When we learn that authentic faith results in freedom and we live within that freedom, other people will want to experience it.

This doesn't mean that we have freedom to do whatever we want. The Bible also addresses that idea.

Read Galatians 5:13. What is it that limits our freedom?

_____ Society's definition of right and wrong

__✗__ God's definition of right and wrong

_____ My personal definition of right and wrong

_____ What seems right at the time

The temptation is to say that we can do anything we want because we are the recipients of God's grace and forgiveness. But living by our standards is disrespectful to God and His Word. The sooner we learn this fact, the better prepared we will be to give a defense of the hope that is within us.

Second, a disciple is a follower. The early disciples followed Jesus from place to place. Today, our following is not a physical following but a following of His teachings. Our following of Jesus' teachings can be observed in our attitudes toward each other. That's what Jesus said in John 13:35. Jesus said that our love for each other will confirm our status as disciples.

If your love for others is an accurate reflection of your status as a disciple, what might someone conclude about you in comparison to Jesus?

_____ I am an accurate reflection of Jesus' love.

__X__ I am an inaccurate reflection of Jesus' love.

What can you do to change this perception?

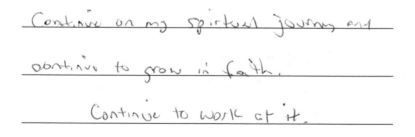

Continue on my spirtual journey and continue to grow in faith.

Continue to work at it.

Read James 2:14–26. What is the proper order for faith and works?

Our faith in God produces good service Deeds

_X_ **Faith produces works.**

____ **Works produce faith.**

Many people believe that they can do good long enough to produce a life of faith. That's backwards. The life of faith produces works that are consistent with biblical principles. Following Jesus Christ results in personal spiritual growth that is realized in the way you think and act. If nothing is changing, you aren't really following Jesus.

The final aspect of discipleship is servanthood. This can be one of the most difficult concepts to grasp. In a world that seeks self-gratification, serving others can be countercultural! That's nothing new.

Read Matthew 20:20–24. In this passage, the mother of James and John wanted her sons to receive places of honor in Jesus' kingdom. Obviously she didn't realize the nature of Jesus' kingdom. James and John didn't understand it either.

Which of the following phrases best characterizes your spiritual life?

_X_ **I am being served.** *It varies at times, try to serve others but sin nature sometimes intervenes*

_X_ **I am serving others by** _being obedient_____ . *to Jesus, God*

73

Look at Jesus' words in Matthew 20:25–28. What was Jesus' reaction to this way of thinking?

Servitude is the Key.

Jesus recognized that even those who followed Him failed to capture His example of servanthood. Some things never change. The ministry of today's church is hampered by believers who wait to be served. The call of discipleship is to service. And this call is for everyone, not a select few.

REACT

So, what is your response? Are you ready to embrace what it means to really be a disciple of Jesus Christ? Until you make this decision, your spiritual life is stalled. You can't move forward without becoming the disciple pictured in Scripture. Let's consider some practical ways to incorporate the truths of this lesson into your life.

The first aspect of being a disciple is that of becoming a learner or a student. List in the following space the things you are doing right now to learn from God and His Word.

attending Bible studies

attending church, Reading the

Bible, Doing service work at the church,

What are some other opportunities available to you?

more service opportunities overall

through the church + New job at

UConn,

The second aspect of being a disciple is that of being a follower of Jesus Christ. Consider your basic life principles. To what extent are they consistent with biblical principles?

_____ Totally consistent

__X__ Mostly consistent

_____ Seldom consistent

_____ Not consistent at all

If necessary, what can you do to improve your response to the previous question?

Not to let anyone or anything get in the way of my spiritual life.

The third aspect of being a disciple is that of being a servant. What are you doing right now to serve God through the ministry of your church?

Helping in the finance team.

What opportunities are available to you?

What excuses have you used to escape God's call for you to serve Him through your church?

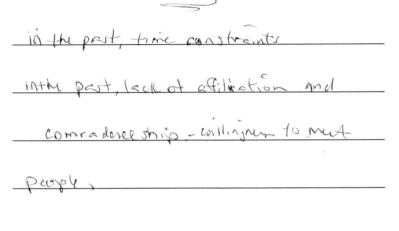

in the past, time constraints

in the past, lack of affiliation and

comradereeship - willingness to meet

people,

You see, the call to discipleship isn't just a call to mental acknowledgment of God's dominion over the world; it is a call to acknowledge God's ownership of every aspect of your life. Until you submit to His ownership, you will never really have the life He intends for you.

> *How often do we fail to hear what God is trying to tell us? To be a disciple is to be a servant.*
>
> BILLY GRAHAM
> *The Journey*

What are three truths you learned in this study, and how will you apply each truth to your daily life?

1. _____

_____

_____

_____

2. _____

_____

_____

_____

3. _____

_____

_____

_____

5

Our
Unfailing
Guide

To GET THE MOST FROM THIS STUDY GUIDE, READ pages 104–113 of *The Journey*.

Faith grows when it is planted in the fertile soil of God's Word. But how can our faith grow stronger?
BILLY GRAHAM
The Journey

THINK ABOUT IT

If you are not guided by God, you will be guided by someone or something else.

—ERIC LIDDELL[1]

Your word is a lamp to my feet and a light for my path.
—PSALM 119:105

When visiting most any popular tourist attraction, you will be given the opportunity to have a guide lead you around the attraction. Some people will take advantage of the availability and skill of the guide; others will make the journey on their own. There are advantages to each approach, so I can't say that one is better than the other.

However, when it comes to matters of faith, a guide isn't optional; it is required. We aren't naturally inclined to embrace the spiritual journey. As a matter of fact, without some help, our spiritual lives will become nothing more than a distant memory. Spiritual growth is as necessary as physical growth. Just like our physical lives need nourishment, our spiritual lives need nourishment, too. That's why we need the help of a guide who can keep us moving in the right direction. Without a guide, we might become disoriented.

REWIND

In the space below, draw a line representing the past year of your spiritual life. Label the areas adjacent to the line using terms such as *wilderness, valley, mountain, desert, detour, oasis, roadblock,* and so forth.

What does the map above reveal to you about your spiritual journey? Who or what have served as your guides along the way?

That their is still alot of work to be done

Debbie, Dennis, Dave, Keith, Vince

It is no surprise that God wants our faith to grow and become stronger. He also has given us the resources necessary to grow. The only thing missing is the desire and commitment to grow.

What are the tools God has given to help you grow spiritually?

X The Bible

X Spiritual leaders

X Your church

X Friends

X Prayer

X Bible-study resources

____ Other: _____

JOURNEY THROUGH GOD'S WORD

Though we are familiar with the Bible, many people don't know how it came into being and why it is in its present form. Of course, the Bible is a collection of writings that have become authoritative in the Christian faith. The Old Testament's thirty-nine books mostly were written in Hebrew and feature three sections—the Law (Genesis, Exodus, Leviticus, Numbers, and Deuteronomy), the Prophets, and the Writings.

The New Testament is made up of twenty-seven books written in Greek and arranged as narrative books (Matthew, Mark, Luke, John, and Acts) and epistles (those written by Paul, other early Christians, and the book of Revelation).

The Old Testament was accepted over time and existed as oral instruction prior to being recorded. Many scholars believe that most of the Old Testament was recorded while the Israelites were in their Babylonian captivity.

The New Testament was well-established by 367 AD, when Athanasius, the bishop of Alexandria, sent an Easter letter advising the churches to accept the twenty-seven books of the modern New Testament as authoritative.

For a book or letter to be considered "God inspired," it had to be widely accepted by the Christian community.

This requirement eliminated from consideration localized instructions that applied to only one specific church or group of people. In addition, the writings had to be proven to be helpful to the Christian community. Finally, the writings had to be valuable when read publicly.[2] By reviewing the history of the development of the modern Bible, it is easy to see how God's hand guided the process. Because of God's guidance, the Bible has become accepted as God's written revelation of Himself. It is not made irrelevant over time and needs no update or revision. The Bible never contradicts itself, and what it says was true remains true. For the Christian community, it is the single most important book in history.

RETHINK

What are some of the tools you use to accomplish your jobs at home or at work?

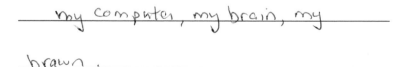

my computer, my brain, my

brawn.

What are the tools you use to accomplish your spiritual goals?

The Bible, Bible Studies, Christian Schoolwork Prayer, Church

---

> *The Bible is essential to our spiritual growth—so essential that lasting spiritual maturity is impossible without it. If our faith isn't rooted in the Bible, it will wither like a plant pulled out of the soil. Only a strong faith—a faith based on God's Word—will protect us from temptation and doubt. Do you want your faith to grow? Then let the Bible begin to saturate your mind and soul.*
>
> BILLY GRAHAM
> *The Journey*

One of the first steps in developing your faith is discovering the value of the Bible. Would you trust your life to a pilot who had not spent time learning to fly the jet on which you are a passenger? Absolutely not! However, by not saturating your mind in biblical truth, you are flying without training.

Spiritual growth must be intentional. Paul said, "Faith comes from hearing the message, and the message is heard through the word of Christ" (Romans 10:17). Maybe you've never heard that verse before, so take a moment to let it sink in. When you hear God's Word, you are drawn to Him in faith. As a result, you crave God's Word, producing more faith. It's an endless cycle for the maturing believer.

How much Scripture would you remember if you had no access to the printed Word of God?

_____ None

___X___ 1–5 verses

_____ More than 5 verses

_____ Complete chapters of books of the Bible

_____ Complete books of the Bible

We have access to the Bible and Bible-study resources today that are unprecedented. Yet, many believers fail to take advantage of these plentiful Bible-study opportunities. Today some believers can't differentiate between popular sayings and biblical truths.

Which of the following statements are actually found in Scripture?

√ God helps those who help themselves.

√ God loves a cheerful giver.

√ Do unto others as you would have them do unto you.

√ Money is the root of all evil.

_____ None of the statements are in the Bible.

√ All of the statements are in the Bible.

Are you surprised at how much or how little Scripture you remember? It's easy for us to take for granted the availability of the Bible. When we take it for granted, we don't place on it the importance it deserves. The Bible is a constant source of power in the life of a believer. But what can you do to avail yourself of that power?

REFLECT

If the Bible was written by real people, why is it called the Word of God? That's been a question skeptics have used in an attempt to discredit the Bible. Yet the Bible answers that question for us.

Read 2 Peter 1:19–21. What makes the Bible unique?

_____ It was written long ago.

__X__ It was written under the inspiration of the Holy Spirit.

_____ It represents the most popular writings of the early church.

_____ The Bible isn't unique; it's just another book.

The Bible is our authority on matters of life and faith. Though the Bible might not address the specifics of every situation we face, it addresses the principles of godly living that are applicable to every area of life. Some people might argue that there are "gray areas" that aren't addressed in the Bible. However, when biblical principles are applied to every decision we make, we will discover that there really are no gray areas. As our authority, the Bible serves as our *guide* to show us how to live and our *instructor* to teach us God's ways.

Which of the following serve as guides or instructors for you?

_____✓_____ Television

_____✓_____ Music

_____ Media

_____✓_____ Books

_____✓_____ Friends

_____✓_____ Other people

_____✓_____ Church

_____✓_____ Scripture

_____ Work/employer

From this list, what are your top three most influential guides or instructors?

Christian Friends, Church, Scripture

_____

_____

Why do you trust these sources?

Because they are what I

consider the most reliable

If we are going to follow Jesus' example, we must view Scripture the way He did. During His wilderness temptations, Jesus relied on the written Word of God to rebuke Satan. Each time He was presented with a temptation, Jesus responded with "for it is written." We might say, "The Bible says . . ." From the very beginning, Satan has been casting doubt on God's instructions.

Rather than question the validity of God's Word against other sources of information, we must establish in our minds the fact that God's Word is the standard against which all other information is judged. This is a subtle shift that makes a huge difference in the way we view life.

Consider some of the controversial issues facing our world today. Has there been a time when these issues were not controversial? If so, what has changed? The change has been in the standards by which these issues are evaluated. What would have happened if these issues would have been consistently evaluated based on the never-changing biblical standards? They would never have become controversial! The issues don't change; only the evaluation criteria change.

So, how can you make the Bible your standard of truth? Let's see what the Bible says to do.

1. *Learn the Bible from others.*

   At the time you experience salvation, you are given one or more spiritual gifts. We'll deal with this concept of spiritual gifts in a future lesson. One of the gifts that is present in the lives of some believers is the gift of teaching.

Read 1 Corinthians 12:27–31. List in the space below the gifts Paul identified.

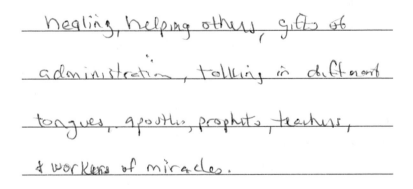

healing, helping others, gifts of
administration, talking in different
tongues, apostles, prophets, teachers,
& workers of miracles.

Don't let the terminology confuse you. *Apostles* is a term for missionaries; *prophets* are those who present the gospel publicly; *teachers* are those who explain biblical truths. You might or might not be gifted in one or more of these areas. If you are, there are responsibilities that accompany your gifts. If not, you have other gifts to be used for God's glory.

How often do you put yourself in a position to learn from others?

Fairly often.

There are many ways to learn from others. Consider these options:

- Bible-study classes at your church or in your community

- Programming through radio and television

- Christian podcasts

- Bible conferences

- Devotional books

- Christian authors

There is great value in joining together with other Christians to study God's Word. Even people who are relatively isolated can come together in "virtual classrooms" to discuss God's Word.

Read Colossians 3:12–17. What does this passage say about joining together for the purposes of spiritual growth?

To show compassion, kindness, gentleness, & patiency. Forgive grievances & Love another. Let the peace of christ rule our hearts.

If I could give only one piece of advice to a new Christian, it would be this: Develop the discipline of spending time alone with God every day. Whether you call it your quiet time or daily devotions or some other term, there is no substitute for a daily time along with God. Set aside a regular time each day, a time when you are fresh and won't be interrupted (even if it's only a few minutes at first). Doesn't God deserve the best minutes of our day?

BILLY GRAHAM
The Journey

---

2. *Learn the Bible on your own.*

Until you accept Jesus Christ as Savior, you will never begin to understand God's Word. Once you have a relationship with God, the Holy Spirit will help you understand and apply the Bible's truths to your everyday life. There is a strategy that will help your personal Bible-study time be more meaning-ful. Let's look at five ways to approach God's Word.

First, come to the Bible joyfully. In its words, the Bible reveals God's love for you. It is something to be excited about. The Bible offers daily advice and guidance that can be trusted. That is something that will keep the joy in your day.

Second, come to the Bible prayerfully and expectantly. When you ask God to speak to you through the Bible, you can expect Him to do so!

Read Psalm 119:18. Rewrite this verse in your own words, and make it a part of your daily prayer before opening God's Word.

Heavenly Father, please allow me to understand and have your word envelope me and lead me to greater things, Amen.

Third, come to the Bible systematically. There are many plans for studying the Bible. Try the following books for starting your journey through God's Word.

_____ **The Gospel of John**

_____ **Acts**

_____ **Psalms**

_____ **Proverbs**

Fourth, come to the Bible thoughtfully. Don't rush through the passage; take time to let its message penetrate your mind. Try reading a verse several times, emphasizing a different word each time. For instance, reading John 3:16 would follow this pattern:

For *God* so loved the world . . .
For God *so* loved the world . . .
For God so *loved* the world . . .
For God so loved the *world* . . .

Finally, come to the Bible obediently. Read the Bible with a commitment to doing what it says.

Read James 1:22. What does this Bible verse say to you?

Don't just read the word, heer what

its saying, and follow it.

REACT

You can't encounter God's Word and walk away unchanged. Even this study has led you to make some decisions about the Bible.

> _God gave the Bible to us because He wants us to know Him and love Him and serve Him. Most of all, He gave it to us so we can become more like Christ._
>
> BILLY GRAHAM
> _The Journey_

What are three truths you learned in this study, and how will you apply each truth to your daily life?

1. Everybody needs guidance to
   lead them in their spiritual journey
   - Listen to what the Bible, pastor, friends,
   are trying to teach.

2. The Bible is ~~God's~~ the most important ~~word devine~~
   book because it is God inspired
   - Learn from + live what is written
   in the Bible .

3. If everybody accepted the Bible
   as the authority on all matters as it
   is todays Social issues would not exist.
   Follow what the Bible teaches when
   making life decision

6

Traveling Together

T̵O GET THE MOST FROM THIS STUDY GUIDE, READ pages 124–133 of *The Journey.*

We not only belong to God, we also belong to each other. We aren't traveling alone on this journey God has given; others are traveling it with us. . . . On this journey we are all brothers and sisters in the same family—the family of God.

BILLY GRAHAM
The Journey

THINK ABOUT IT

Fellowship is fundamental to mission! Commitment to Christ, commitment to each other in Christ, is prerequisite to authentic Christian witness.

—RICHARD C. HALVERSON[1]

For where two or three come together in my name, there am I with them.

—MATTHEW 18:20

At a time in our history when individualism is a popular philosophy, it might strike you as odd that we would promote the collaborative nature of the Christian faith. Yet, that is exactly how the Bible describes faith in God. The Christian life is not lived out in isolation; it is lived out in community.

The family of God consists of the universal fellowship of like-minded believers in Jesus Christ. When you accept Jesus Christ as Savior, you become a part of the family of God. You then choose to identify with a local body of believers that we call the church. Within the church, you become a part of small-group Bible studies and ministries that help you grow and serve God faithfully. This is all part of God's plan; we need each other!

REWIND

List the people who are most supportive and helpful in your spiritual life.

Dennis, Debbie, Debbie, & Vince

the entire BBSG

What are the settings in which you interact with these people?

Bible study, home, church

Your choice to give your life to Jesus Christ is a personal choice. No one can do it for you, and you don't become a believer based on the faith of your parents, grandparents, siblings, or other people. But once you become a Christian, those people and other believers are vital to your spiritual growth.

> _A solitary Christian is almost a contradiction, because we each are part of a larger whole. Just as there is something wrong when a brother or sister becomes alienated from the rest of their family, so there is something wrong when Christians refuse to have anything to do with their fellow Christians. We are on this journey together, and God wants us to live the Christian life together._
>
> BILLY GRAHAM
> _The Journey_

What is the difference between church membership and salvation?

↘ *B. G. Version.*

_____ There is no difference; they are the same. *Possibly*

_____ You must be a church member to be saved.

↘
_____ You must be saved to be a church member.

✔︎ Church membership isn't a biblical concept.

_____ Other

JOURNEY THROUGH GOD'S WORD

In the Old Testament times, there was a close connection between government and faith. Before Israel had a king, it was a theocracy—that is, it was ruled by a religious authority. Eventually, the religious and political aspects of the nation separated. There were times during which the religious leaders worked alongside the political leaders and times during which the two elements of Israelite life were separate.

In the early New Testament period, the Roman government didn't pay much attention to the small but growing group of believers. Jesus, however, urged His followers to be good citizens and to pay their taxes. As the Christian

---

faith grew, the Roman government became more and more concerned about its influence. It wasn't long before the Roman Empire was very aware of—and hostile toward—the Christians within its borders.

According to the Bible, ultimately all governmental authorities are under God's control. In Jeremiah 27:5–6, God declared His power over all earthly powers. When Jesus was before Pilate immediately prior to His crucifixion, Jesus declared God's dominion over Pilate and the Jewish leaders who delivered Him to be killed (John 19:11). In Romans 13:1, Paul described the authoritative hierarchy by describing the governing authorities as having been established by God.

Because all governmental authorities are established by God, there can be no separation of faith and government. However, some civil authorities might choose differing degrees of control over organized religion. Regardless of the actions of the government, Christians are instructed to be good citizens (1 Timothy 2:1–2) while positively influencing their culture with biblical values and principles.[2] It is the responsibility of all Christians to work peacefully to keep biblical principles at the heart of every aspect of their lives. In doing so, society will be positively affected as God works through the lives of believers who are good citizens.

RETHINK

What is the first thing that comes to mind when you think about the word *church*?

Fellowship

If someone asked you to explain *church*, how would you respond?

A gathering of believers coming together to share their spiritual journey

Even though it is a very familiar term, there is a lot of confusion about the meaning of *church*. For some people, the church is a building in which they meet together for worship. For others, the church is the administrative and authoritative element of their particular denomination. Others see the church as a place to meet people and participate in social activities. Still others view the church as their particular congregation.

If we are going to be involved in the church, we need to have a biblically based understanding about what it really is.

Read the following Scriptures and mark each one with either 1 or 2, with 1 representing "a local group of Christians" and 2 representing "the company of all believers." [Answers can be found at the end of this chapter.]

____1____ Acts 1:8

____1____ Acts 13:1

____1____ 1 Corinthians 1:2

____2____ Ephesians 5:23

According to the Bible, the "church" has two basic meanings—a local group of Christians and the company of all believers. When the church was first organized, small groups of Christ-followers met together in homes to pray, learn, and encourage one another. These small, home-based groups are the predecessors to the modern church congregation.

The advent of the congregation had one downside—each small group of believers practiced its faith in ways that might have varied from the practices of other small groups. This variance in practice is part of the reason some New Testament writers addressed the relationship between different small groups. The message was (and remains) that "the church" is the collective body of believers from all over the world. The church isn't limited to a particular denomination or church.

REFLECT

Why do Christians need to be in spiritual relationships with each other? God has given us to each other. We are mutually beneficial to one another when we purpose together to accomplish God's work.

Read Proverbs 27:17. What does this verse say about our roles in the lives of other believers?

to strengthen one another.

Is the desire to go to church a requirement for salvation? No, it is a result of an authentic relationship with God. You don't go to church in order to be saved; you desire the fellowship of other believers because you are saved. The Bible isn't silent on this issue. Scripture offers four reasons why we are to be a part of a local congregation.

1. **We should come together to worship God.**
   In the Old Testament, God's people gathered together to praise God for His goodness and provision. In the New Testament, we are instructed to

worship God together. Nowhere in Scripture does it
tell us to isolate ourselves from other believers.

Read Psalm 100:4. What is the basic message of this verse?

To praise + thank the Lord together
in worship.

Read Colossians 3:16. What should our worship of God include?

teaching + admonishing with wisdom
Singing of Psalms, songs, + hymns with
gratitude to God.

So, why do we have differing styles of worship and church practice? In worship, one style doesn't suit all people. Worship is
intended to turn your attention toward God. For some people,
that means a very calm, reflective worship service. For others,
their hearts are turned to God with more upbeat, contemporary
worship. Some prefer smaller congregations; others enjoy larger

gatherings. In the end, the ultimate question is "Does your worship turn your heart toward God in worship and praise?" If the answer to that question is yes, then where you are worshiping is right for you.

How do you respond to worship styles that are different from the way you worship at your church?

_____ The way our church does it is right; everything else is wrong.

_____ I tolerate other styles but don't get anything out of them.

_X_ I can worship no matter what style of worship the church uses.

_____ I've never experienced any worship style other than mine.

What do you believe is God's concern when you worship?

_____ He is concerned about the style of worship.

_____ He is concerned about the place of worship.

_____ He is concerned about my comfort in worship.

_X_ He is concerned about the attitude of my heart during worship.

Contrary to what some people believe, worship isn't entertainment. We come together to enjoy God's presence, not the show. In real worship, God is the audience and we are the performers.

Read John 4:23. What type of person is God seeking?

The kind that worship in Spirit & truth.

2. **We should come together to hear God's Word.**
   When we hear someone else explain God's Word, we get a fresh perspective on it. We might be challenged, encouraged, instructed, or chastised through the proclamation and teaching that occurs when we gather together with other believers. Two of the spiritual gifts are preaching and teaching (Ephesians 4:11).

Think about your spiritual journey. Who have been the most influential preachers and teachers?

Keith, Cathy, Debbie, AA, Dave
Micky Cunbel

Reread Colossians 3:16. What does this verse say about the role of God's Word in your life?

that the word + should dwell in us

richly.

Which of the following opportunities to engage in the study of God's Word are a regular part of your spiritual journey?

_X_ Hearing God's Word from a preacher

_X_ Participating in small-group Bible studies

_____ Attending special conferences and events

_____ Attending retreats

Are you satisfied with your efforts to learn God's Word? Why or why not?

Not completely, I can always do

more + make more time for God.

Some of my greatest encouragement over the years has come from godly friends who were willing to pray and share their wisdom with me. Whenever we are with other believers—whether in a church service with hundreds of people or just sharing a cup of coffee with a Christian friend—God can lift us up and increase our faith through their encouragement and counsel.

BILLY GRAHAM
The Journey

3. **We should come together to encourage one another.** We all have problems and need other people to help us deal with them. Yet, many times people turn to advisors who do not share their love for God's Word.

What is the danger of seeking advice from people who are not believers?

bad advice. Non-Spiritual not Gods will

When it comes to seeking help for your problems, where do you immediately turn?

My wife + Denna + Debbie,

When you read Hebrews 10:25, you discover that God's desire is that we make meeting together a priority. One of the purposes of worship is encouraging other people.

Think about situations in which you have been encouraged. Which of the following have been used to encourage you?

_×_ A pat on the back

_×_ A smile

_×_ The Bible

_×_ A sermon

_×_ A Bible-study lesson

_×_ Prayer

_×_ A kind word

_×_ A door being held open for you

Read Hebrews 3:13 and 1 Thessalonians 5:11. What are some "small things" you can do to encourage others?

Encourage one another daily &

build each other up.

4. **We should come together so we can reach out to others with Christ's love.**

   We sometimes get the idea that we have to repair our lives before we can come to God. Nothing could be more untrue; we come to God so He can repair our lives. That means there are hurting and broken people sitting near you every time you gather with fellow believers. Maybe you've been one of those people.

As believers, we have the responsibility to tell others about God's love for them. We also have the responsibility to be an example of what God can do in the lives of those He has redeemed.

Read Ephesians 4:12. What are you doing to serve God and lead others to Him?

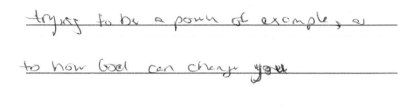

trying to be a power of example, as to how God can change you

REACT

It's obvious that you need to be involved in a local church, but how do you find one? Here are a few things to consider when choosing a congregation in which you can become an active participant.

1. Is the church led by reliable leaders? (2 Timothy 2:2).

2. Seek the counsel of other Christians.

3. Evaluate your needs and those of your family, and compare them to the offerings of the church.

4. Evaluate the educational ministry of the church.

5. Ask yourself, *What is the church doing to make a difference in its community and the world?*

6. Look for where God is at work, and invest your resources there.

7. Pray, asking God to guide you to the place that is right for you.

Don't take this journey God has given you alone. God is with you, and so are His people. You need them—and they need you.

BILLY GRAHAM
The Journey

What are three truths you learned in this study, and how will you apply each truth to your daily life?

1. _____

_____

_____

_____

2. _____

_____

_____

_____

3. _____

_____

_____

_____

Answers to Scripture matching on page 107 —

(1) Acts 1:8; (1) Acts 13:1; (1) 1 Corinthians 1:2; (2) Ephesians 5:23

NOTES

- Let your commitment to Christ guide your conduct.

- Focus on God, not on your problems.

CHAPTER 1

1. Bob Kelly, *Worth Repeating*, 2003. Grand Rapids, MI: Kregel Publications, 322.

CHAPTER 2

1. Bob Kelly, *Worth Repeating*, 246.
2. *Holman Illustrated Bible Dictionary*, 2003. Nashville, TN: B&H, 425–426.

CHAPTER 3

1. Bob Kelly, *Worth Repeating*, 160.
2. *Holman Illustrated Bible Dictionary*, 425–426.

CHAPTER 4

1. Bob Kelly, *Worth Repeating*, 86.

CHAPTER 5

1. Bob Kelly, *Worth Repeating*, 161.
2. *Holman Illustrated Bible Dictionary*, 200–202.

CHAPTER 6

1. Bob Kelly, *Worth Repeating*, 121.
2. *Holman Illustrated Bible Dictionary*, 297–298.

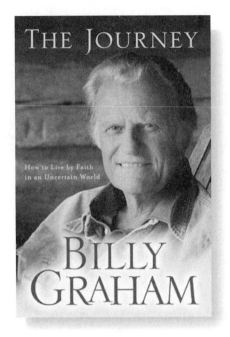

Billy Graham is respected and loved around the world. *The Journey* is his magnum opus, the culmination of a lifetime of experience and ministry. With insight that comes only from a life spent with God, this book is filled with wisdom, encouragement, hope, and inspiration for anyone who wants to live a happier, more fulfilling life.

978-0-8499-1887-2 (PB)